THE LOST LETTERS

— OF THE —

AMERICAN REVOLUTION

TEACHER'S EDITION

Instructor's Guide for
Secondary & Postsecondary Classrooms

ELIZABETH WINSLOW

The Lost Letters of the American Revolution

Collected, Transcribed, and Introduced by
Elizabeth Winslow

With Full Editorial Notes and Historical Commentary

ISBN: 979-8-9931646-2-5

Printed in the United States of America

For permissions and inquiries, contact:

Elizabeth Winslow Publishing

www.elizabethwinslowpublishing.com

At a Glance: Adoption & Instructional Use

This curriculum companion is intentionally designed for flexible adoption across multiple educational settings. The chart below provides a quick reference for how instructors, facilitators, and families may implement the material, including which companion texts are most appropriate for each setting.

Setting	Recommended Use	Most Appropriate Companion Book
Upper-Level High School	High School Track core units with optional experiential enrichment	The Lost Letters of the American Revolution (core)
AP/Dual Enrollment	Combined High School and University Tracks with seminar-style discussion	The Lost Letters of the American Revolution (core); selected excerpts from Lost Recipes of the American Revolution (*optional*)
Homeschool Program	Required core curriculum with Independent / At-Home enrichment options	The Lost Letters of the American Revolution (core); Lost Recipes of the American Revolution for experiential, project-based learning
Undergraduate Studies	University Track with analytical writing and a capstone project	The Lost Letters of the American Revolution (core); Lost Recipes of the American Revolution for material culture analysis (optional)

All formats are adaptable for synchronous, asynchronous, classroom-based, seminar, or independent study environments. Experiential components are optional and may be adapted to suit instructional goals, facilities, and learner needs.

CONTENTS

INTRODUCTION FOR EDUCATORS, FACILITATORS, AND FAMILIES

This Instructor & Student Curriculum Companion was created to support the use of *The Lost Letters of the American Revolution* as a primary-source learning resource across a wide range of educational environments. It is designed for use in upper-level High School Track (Grades 10–12), dual enrollment, homeschool, and undergraduate settings.

At its core, this curriculum centers on authentic letters written during the Revolutionary era. These letters are treated as historical evidence, allowing students to engage directly with the voices of soldiers, civilians, family members, and witnesses to America's founding. Rather than encountering the Revolution solely through retrospective narrative, learners encounter history as it was experienced in real time—marked by uncertainty, sacrifice, resilience, and deeply personal decision-making.

Instruction throughout the companion emphasizes essential historical thinking skills, including contextual analysis, perspective-taking, evaluating bias, and interpreting emotional language as evidence. The audiobook format supports auditory learners, students with print-access challenges, ESL learners, and those participating in remote or asynchronous instruction, while all written activities may be used independently of audio when needed.

To accommodate varied instructional needs, the curriculum is structured around required core components and clearly labeled optional enrichment pathways. Required materials focus exclusively on *The Lost Letters of the American Revolution* and may be used independently in any instructional setting. Optional enrichment activities draw from *Lost Recipes of the American*

Revolution and are framed as explorations of material culture and daily life, supporting deeper engagement with social and cultural history.

All enrichment activities are optional and adaptable. Cooking is never required, and no activity assumes access to specialized facilities. Where experiential options are included, they are designed for independent, at-home, instructor-led, or group-based learning, at the educator's or family's discretion.

University Track Level Course Adoption Overview

At the undergraduate level, this curriculum companion is appropriate for use in introductory and upper-division courses in American history, early American studies, humanities, and related interdisciplinary fields. The curriculum emphasizes close reading, analytical writing, seminar-style discussion, and primary-source interpretation aligned with **University Track**-level expectations.

University Track activities encourage students to evaluate emotional language, uncertainty, and personal perspective as legitimate historical evidence, moving beyond celebratory or retrospective narratives of the Revolutionary era. Assessment options support analytical essays, seminar leadership, comparative source analysis, and capstone-style projects appropriate for survey courses, honors sections, and independent study.

This companion may be adopted as a core instructional text, a supplemental seminar resource, or a modular primary-source reader within larger survey courses. Its structure supports both synchronous and asynchronous instruction and aligns well with learning outcomes commonly associated with undergraduate history programs.

Recommended For

This curriculum companion is appropriate for:

- Upper-level High School Track history courses (Grades 10–12)

- Dual enrollment and AP-aligned coursework

- Undergraduate history, humanities, and American studies courses

- Public history, museum studies, and archival studies programs

- Homeschool learners seeking transcript-worthy coursework

- Independent study and lifelong learning programs

Each instructional unit includes:

- Core curriculum aligned with historical standards

- Clearly differentiated High School Track and **University Track** learning tracks

- Instructor guidance and suggested assessment options

- Optional experiential enrichment is clearly labeled throughout

Units may be taught sequentially or selectively, and instructors may adjust pacing or depth to suit their course structure. This flexibility allows the curriculum to function effectively in semester-long courses, multi-week thematic units, enrichment programs, or independent study.

The purpose of this companion is not to prescribe a single method of instruction, but to provide adaptable, academically rigorous tools that honor historical integrity while meeting the realities of contemporary education.

HOW TO USE THIS COMPANION

Quick Start Guide

This section provides practical steps for implementing the curriculum in a variety of instructional settings. It may be used in full or in part, depending on instructional goals, time constraints, and learning environment.

Step 1: Select Your Core Content

Begin with *The Lost Letters of the American Revolution,* **the** required core text for all instructional units.

Each unit includes:

- Assigned listening or reading segments
- Student-facing discussion questions
- Instructor notes and assessment options

These components may be used independently of any enrichment activities.

Step 2: Choose the Appropriate Learning Track

Each unit provides two clearly labeled instructional tracks:

- High School Track (Grades 10–12 / AP / Dual Enrollment)
- Guided analysis, scaffolded discussion, and structured prompts
- **University Track** (Undergraduate)
- Advanced analysis, interpretive questions, and seminar-style discussion

Instructors, facilitators, or families may select the track that best fits their learners. Dual-enrollment and advanced secondary courses may draw from both.

Step 3: Decide on Learning Format

All core activities are adaptable for:

- Traditional classroom instruction
- Homeschool education
- Online or asynchronous courses
- Independent study or library-led learning

Listening assignments may be completed individually or collectively. Written activities may be submitted digitally or discussed orally, as appropriate.

Step 4: Use Optional Enrichment as Desired

Optional enrichment activities are clearly labeled and may be used at the instructor's or family's discretion. These extensions draw from *Lost Recipes of the American Revolution* and explore historical material culture and daily life.

Two enrichment formats are provided:

- Independent / At-Home Extensions

- Suitable for homeschool, online, and self-paced learning

- Instructor-Led / Group Extensions

- Suitable for in-person, hybrid, or seminar-style courses

Cooking **is** never required, and all enrichment activities may be adapted, modified, or omitted.

Step 5: Select Assessment Options

Each unit includes suggested assessment options for both learning levels. Instructors may choose to:

- Assign short written responses

- Facilitate discussions or presentations

- Use primary-source analysis essays

- Incorporate reflective or comparative assignments

Assessments are designed to support historical thinking skills rather than rote memorization.

Step 6: Adapt as Needed

This companion is intentionally non-prescriptive. Educators and families are encouraged to:

- Use only selected units

- Adjust pacing or depth

- Combine tracks for mixed-ability learners

The goal is historical understanding through authentic voices, supported by adaptable instructional tools.

Need Less or More?

This companion may support:

- Single-unit lessons

- Multi-week thematic units

- Semester-long courses

- Independent or enrichment study

Adapt the content to fit your needs.

CURRICULUM ALIGNMENT OVERVIEW

High School Track Alignment

This companion supports instruction in:

- AP U.S. History

- Honors U.S. History

- Dual Enrollment U.S. History

Skills emphasized:

- Primary-source analysis

- Historical empathy and perspective

- Evidence-based writing

- Contextual interpretation

UNIVERSITY TRACK ALIGNMENT

This companion supports:

- U.S. History I
- Colonial America
- Revolutionary War Studies
- American Studies / Humanities

Skills emphasized:

- Source criticism
- Narrative versus lived experience
- Social and material culture analysis
- Interpretive discussion and writing

REQUIRED CORE CURRICULUM

(All Educational Settings)

The core curriculum focuses exclusively on *The Lost Letters of the American Revolution* and may be used without any enrichment activities.

Each unit includes:

- Assigned listening or reading segments
- Student-facing discussion questions
- Instructor guidance
- Suggested assessments

UNIT 1

Voices on the Eve of Revolution

Historical Focus

- Rising tension in the colonies

- Loyalty, uncertainty, and fear

- Civilian and military perspectives

Instructional Note

This unit introduces students to primary-source analysis by examining uncertainty, perspective, and emotional language as historical evidence.

Suggested Listening

Approximately 45–60 minutes, selected letters from the early period of unrest leading into open conflict.

Student Discussion Guide

◇ **High School Track: *What concerns or fears appear most frequently in these letters?***

1. How do writers describe daily life as tensions increase?

2. Do the writers expect war to bring clarity or uncertainty? What words or phrases in the letters support your answer?

◇ **University Track: *How do expectations of conflict differ by social role (soldier, civilian, family member)?***

1. In what ways do these letters complicate traditional narratives of patriotic certainty?

2. How does private correspondence differ from public political rhetoric of the same period, and why does that distinction matter historically?

OPTIONAL EXPERIENTIAL ENRICHMENT

Material Culture & Lived Experience

(Clearly Optional – Not Required)

This extension supports learners—especially homeschool, online, and independent students—in experiencing history as it unfolded in real time, without requiring cooking or group settings.

◇ Option A — Independent / At-Home

(Homeschool, Online, Independent Study)

Experiential Letter Immersion

Students may:

- Select one letter from the unit
- Read or listen to it twice:
  - First, for general understanding
  - Second, focusing on emotional tone and uncertainty

Then complete one of the following:

Choice 1: Letter Reflection

Write a short reflection answering:

What does the writer not know yet, and how does that uncertainty shape their tone?

Choice 2: Perspective Journal

Write a one-page journal entry from the writer's perspective, one week after the letter was written, imagining what fears or questions remain unresolved.

No reenactment, costumes, or cooking are required.

This activity emphasizes empathy, inference, and historical imagination grounded in evidence.

◊ Option B — Instructor-Led / Group

(In-Person or Seminar Courses)

Students may:

- Read or listen to letters aloud

- Identify phrases that reveal fear, hesitation, or hope

- Discuss how uncertainty challenges modern expectations of historical "confidence."

This option works well as a seminar discussion or Socratic-style conversation.

ASSESSMENT OPTIONS

◊ High School Track

- Short primary-source response paper

- Guided comparison between a letter and a textbook account of the same period

◊ University Track

- Analytical essay using emotional language as historical evidence

- Seminar discussion leadership assignment

Instructional Rationale

This unit balances accessibility with academic rigor by introducing primary-source analysis without overloading students. It is designed to function effectively in homeschool, online, evening, and independent-learning environments while maintaining evidence-based historical inquiry.

UNIT 2

WAR REACHES THE HOME FRONT

Historical Focus

- The impact of war on civilians and families

- Separation, fear, and endurance

- Women's voices and domestic responsibility

- The collapse of boundaries between battlefield and home

Instructional Note

This unit expands primary-source analysis by examining how war reshapes daily life, emotional labor, and family roles, particularly for those not serving as soldiers.

Suggested Listening

Approximately 45–60 minutes, selected letters describing civilian life, family correspondence, and the domestic consequences of the Revolutionary conflict.

Student Discussion Guide

⬦ **High School Track**

1. How does the tone of letters written from home differ from those written by soldiers?

2. What new responsibilities do family members take on as the war continues?

3. What emotions appear most frequently in these letters, and why?

◇ **University Track**

In what ways do these letters challenge the idea that civilians were separate from the war effort?

1. How do gender expectations appear reinforced, adapted, or strained in these letters?

2. What forms of labor—emotional, domestic, and economic—are revealed through private correspondence?

INSTRUCTOR NOTES

- Emphasize emotional labor as a historical force, not a private footnote.

- Encourage students to consider domestic spaces as sites of endurance, resistance, and continuity.

- This unit works well for introducing social history **and** women's history through primary sources.

REQUIRED CORE ANALYSIS ACTIVITY

Letters as Historical Evidence

Students select one letter and analyze it using the following framework:

- Author: Who is writing, and what is their role in the household or community?

- Audience: Who is the intended recipient, and why?

- Context: What pressures—economic, emotional, or social—shape this letter?

- Emotion: How does emotional language function as evidence of wartime strain?

Students should support their analysis with specific language from the text.

OPTIONAL EXPERIENTIAL ENRICHMENT

Domestic Life, Labor & Survival

This enrichment supports homeschoolers, online learners, and instructors seeking deeper engagement with daily life on the home front, using *Lost Recipes of the American Revolution* as material culture evidence.

◇ Option A — Independent / At-Home

(Homeschool, Online, Independent Study)

Home Front Immersion Activity

Students may complete one of the following:

Choice 1: Daily Life Reconstruction

- Identify references to chores, food preparation, caregiving, or household management in the letters.

- Write a short narrative describing a single day in the life of the letter writer or recipient.

Choice 2: Recipe as Evidence (No Cooking Required)

- Examine a simple, everyday recipe from *Lost Recipes of the American Revolution*.

- Identify what the recipe suggests about:
  - Ingredient access
  - Time and labor
  - Wartime scarcity

- Write a reflection connecting the recipe to the emotional tone of the letters.

◇ OPTION B — INSTRUCTOR-LED / GROUP

(In-Person, Hybrid, or Seminar Courses)

Students may:

- Compare letters describing household strain with a domestic recipe

- Discuss how food preparation reflects gender roles, class, and economic pressure

- Analyze how "ordinary" tasks become historically significant during war

Cooking, if used, is optional and at the instructor's discretion.

ASSESSMENT OPTIONS

◇ **High School Track**

- Short essay: *How war reshapes family roles*

- Primary-source response focused on civilian experience

◇ **University Track**

- Analytical paper on the home front as a site of wartime labor

- Seminar discussion on leadership, gender, and domestic survival

UNIT 2 LEARNING OUTCOMES

By the end of this unit, students should be able to:

- Explain how war affected civilians beyond the battlefield

- Identify emotional and domestic labor as historical evidence

- Analyze letters as sources of social and gender history

- Connect lived experience to broader Revolutionary narratives

UNIT 3

SCARCITY, SURVIVAL, AND SUPPLY

Historical Focus

- Food shortages and rationing
- Disruption of supply chains
- Military versus civilian access to resources
- Regional and class-based differences in survival
- The relationship between morale and material conditions

Instructional Note

This unit develops students' ability to analyze material conditions—such as food availability and supply—as historical evidence, connecting emotion, economy, and survival during the Revolutionary era.

Suggested Listening

Approximately 45–60 minutes, selected letters describing shortages, hunger, rationing, supply problems, and the physical realities of sustaining life during wartime.

STUDENT DISCUSSION GUIDE

What evidence of scarcity appears most frequently in these letters?

High School Track

1. How do shortages affect morale, decision-making, or family life?
2. Who seems most affected by the lack of food or supplies, and why?

University Track

1. How do these letters reveal weaknesses or breakdowns in Revolutionary supply systems?

2. In what ways does scarcity expose class, regional, or military privilege?

3. How does the language of hunger or deprivation function as historical evidence rather than metaphor?

INSTRUCTOR NOTES

This unit is particularly effective for examining material culture and survival during the Revolutionary era. Instructors may find it useful for helping students connect emotional language in letters with the physical realities of wartime scarcity and supply disruption.

Optional enrichment activities in this unit support independent, online, and homeschool learners especially well, while also offering opportunities for deeper material-culture analysis in undergraduate settings. Instructors may choose to emphasize letters, recipes, or both, depending on course goals and available instructional time.

This unit reinforces the study of history as lived experience—shaped by access, adaptation, and endurance—rather than focusing solely on abstract political outcomes.

REQUIRED CORE ANALYSIS ACTIVITY

Supply as Historical Evidence

Students select one letter from this unit and analyze it using the following framework:

- What is missing or scarce?

- Who is affected by this scarcity?

- What substitutions, solutions, or adaptations are mentioned or implied?

- How does scarcity influence tone, urgency, or emotion?

Students should support their analysis with specific language from the letter.

OPTIONAL EXPERIENTIAL ENRICHMENT

Foodways, Substitution, and Survival

This enrichment draws from *Lost Recipes of the American Revolution* to examine how people adapted to shortages using ingenuity, substitution, and necessity. Cooking is never required.

Option A — Independent/At-Home

(Homeschool, Online, Independent Study)

Students complete one of the following activities:

Choice 1: Recipe Analysis Under Constraint

- Examine a wartime or everyday recipe from *Lost Recipes of the American Revolution*.

- Identify which ingredients were likely difficult to obtain.

- Note any substitutions or simplifications.

Reflection Prompt:

How does this recipe demonstrate adaptation rather than abundance?

Choice 2: Letter-to-Recipe Connection

- Pair one letter describing scarcity with one recipe.

- Write a short analysis explaining how each source reveals survival strategies in different ways.

Option B — Instructor-Led / Group

(In-Person, Hybrid, or Seminar Courses)

Students may:

- Compare letters describing hunger or shortages with recipes built around limited ingredients

- Discuss how scarcity affects morale, social hierarchy, and military effectiveness

- Analyze substitution as a form of resilience and endurance

Cooking, if used, is optional and at the instructor's discretion.

ASSESSMENT OPTIONS

High School Track

- Short essay: *How scarcity shaped daily life during the American Revolution*

- Document-based response connecting letters to material conditions

University Track

- Analytical paper on wartime supply systems using letters as primary evidence

- Seminar discussion leadership focused on scarcity as a driver of social change.

UNIT 3 LEARNING OUTCOMES

By the end of this unit, students should be able to:

- Explain how scarcity affected civilians and soldiers differently

- Analyze food and supply as interconnected historical systems

- Use letters and recipes as complementary primary sources

- Connect material conditions to emotional, social, and political outcomes

UNIT 4

SOLDIERS' DAILY LIFE, MORALE, AND ENDURANCE

Historical Focus

- Daily routines of soldiers during the Revolutionary War
- Physical hardship, illness, and exhaustion
- Morale, discipline, and perseverance
- The emotional distance between battlefield experience and home
- Survival beyond battles

Instructional Note

This unit develops students' understanding of military life by examining soldiers' daily experiences as revealed through personal correspondence, emphasizing endurance, morale, and the realities of sustained conflict.

Suggested Listening

Approximately 45–60 minutes, selected letters written by soldiers describing camp life, marches, illness, hunger, fatigue, and emotional strain.

STUDENT DISCUSSION GUIDE

High School Track

1. What aspects of daily military life appear most frequently in these letters?

2. How do soldiers describe physical hardship and exhaustion?

3. What seems to sustain morale during difficult conditions?

University Track

1. How do these letters complicate traditional narratives of heroism and military glory?

2. In what ways do daily routines function as tools of discipline and survival?

3. How does correspondence shape soldiers' emotional endurance?

Instructor Notes

This unit allows students to examine war not as a series of battles, but as a sustained human experience defined by routine, deprivation, and resilience. Letters provide insight into how soldiers endured long periods of hardship between moments of combat.

Optional enrichment activities support independent and online learners while offering opportunities for deeper analysis in undergraduate courses. Instructors may emphasize emotional endurance, military discipline, or the contrast between expectation and reality, depending on course goals.

This unit reinforces the idea that survival, rather than victory alone, shaped the Revolutionary War experience.

REQUIRED CORE ANALYSIS ACTIVITY

Endurance as Historical Evidence

Students select one letter and analyze it using the following framework:

- What daily hardships are described?

- How does the writer express fatigue, fear, or perseverance?

- What role do routine, discipline, or hope play in survival?

- How does the letter redefine what it meant to "serve" during the war?

Students should support their analysis with specific language from the letter.

OPTIONAL EXPERIENTIAL ENRICHMENT

Military Life, Routine, and Survival

This enrichment draws from *Lost Recipes of the American Revolution* and related material culture to examine how soldiers sustained themselves physically and mentally. Cooking is never required.

Option A — Independent / At-Home

(Homeschool, Online, Independent Study)

Students complete one of the following:

Choice 1: Camp Life Reconstruction

- Identify references to food, shelter, illness, or daily routine in the letters.

- Write a one-page narrative describing a typical day in camp based on the evidence provided.

Choice 2: Rations as Evidence

- Examine a simple ration-based recipe or food description from *Lost Recipes of the American Revolution.*

- Analyze what it reveals about nutrition, morale, and endurance.

Option B — Instructor-Led / Group

(In-Person, Hybrid, or Seminar Courses)

Students may:

- Compare soldiers' letters with ration descriptions or camp records

- Discuss how routine and discipline contributed to survival

- Analyze how deprivation affected morale and identity

Any hands-on activity is optional and instructor-directed.

ASSESSMENT OPTIONS

High School Track

- Short essay: *How daily hardship shaped soldiers' endurance*

- Primary-source response focused on camp life

University Track

- Analytical paper on morale and endurance in Revolutionary armies

- Seminar discussion leadership examining routine as a survival strategy

UNIT 4 LEARNING OUTCOMES

By the end of this unit, students should be able to:

- Describe the daily realities of military life during the Revolution

- Analyze endurance and morale as historical forces

- Interpret letters as evidence of sustained hardship

- Connect routine and survival to broader military outcomes

UNIT 5

LOYALTY, DIVISION, AND IDENTITY

Historical Focus

- Divided loyalties among colonists

- Patriot, Loyalist, and undecided perspectives

- Family, community, and regional conflict

- The personal cost of choosing sides

- Identity formation during the Revolution

Instructional Note

This unit examines how loyalty and identity were contested during the Revolutionary era, revealing the Revolution as a civil conflict that fractured families, communities, and personal relationships.

Suggested Listening

Approximately 45–60 minutes, selected letters reflecting divided loyalties, political uncertainty, shifting allegiances, and the personal consequences of choosing—or refusing to choose—a side.

STUDENT DISCUSSION GUIDE

High School Track

1. What different viewpoints about the Revolution appear in these letters?

2. How do writers describe conflict within families or communities?

3. What risks are associated with expressing loyalty to either side?

University Track

1. How do these letters complicate the idea of a unified revolutionary identity?

2. In what ways does loyalty function as both a political and personal decision?

3. How do writers negotiate identity when allegiances are uncertain or dangerous?

INSTRUCTOR NOTES

This unit encourages students to move beyond simplified narratives of Patriot versus Loyalist by examining the Revolution as a period of deep internal division. Letters reveal how identity was shaped not only by ideology, but by geography, family ties, economic dependency, and personal survival.

Optional enrichment activities support independent and online learners while offering opportunities for advanced discussion in undergraduate courses. Instructors may emphasize political ideology, social pressure, or moral ambiguity, depending on instructional goals.

This unit reinforces the understanding of Revolution as a human process marked by conflict, hesitation, and consequences.

REQUIRED CORE ANALYSIS ACTIVITY

Loyalty as Historical Evidence

Students select one letter and analyze it using the following framework:

- What position or hesitation does the writer express regarding the conflict?

- What factors influence the writer's sense of loyalty (family, safety, belief, economy)?

- What risks or consequences are acknowledged or implied?

- How does the letter reflect the instability of identity during the Revolution?

Students should support their analysis with specific language from the letter.

OPTIONAL EXPERIENTIAL ENRICHMENT

CHOICE, CONSEQUENCE, AND BELONGING

This enrichment supports deeper engagement with questions of loyalty, identity, and belonging, using letters and material culture to explore lived experience. Cooking is never required.

Option A — Independent / At-Home

(Homeschool, Online, Independent Study)

Students complete one of the following activities:

Choice 1: Journal Decision

- Choose one letter from the unit.

- Write a journal entry from the writer's perspective explaining the pressures influencing their loyalty or uncertainty.

Choice 2: Identity Mapping

- Create a written or visual map identifying the factors that shape a writer's identity (family, location, occupation, beliefs).

- Accompany the map with a short explanation supported by letter evidence.

Option B — Instructor-Led / Group

(In-Person, Hybrid, or Seminar Courses)

Students may:

- Compare letters expressing different allegiances
- Discuss how social pressure influences political identity
- Analyze moral ambiguity and risk in revolutionary decision-making

Group activities may be discussion-based and do not require reenactment.

ASSESSMENT OPTIONS

High School Track

- Short essay: *How loyalty divided communities during the American Revolution*
- Primary-source response focused on identity and choice

University Track

- Analytical paper on loyalty as a social and political construct
- Seminar discussion on the leadership of internal conflict during the Revolution

UNIT 5 LEARNING OUTCOMES

By the end of this unit, students should be able to:

- Explain how loyalty was contested during the Revolutionary era
- Analyze identity as a fluid and situational concept
- Interpret letters as evidence of social and political division
- Recognize the Revolution as a civil conflict as well as a war for independence

UNIT 6

ESPIONAGE, SECRECY, AND TRUST

Historical Focus

- Intelligence gathering during the Revolutionary War
- Secret correspondence and coded language
- Trust, betrayal, and risk
- Information as power
- The dangers of communication in wartime

Instructional Note

This unit explores how secrecy, intelligence, and trust shaped the Revolutionary War by examining letters written with caution, concealment, and strategic intent.

Suggested Listening

Approximately 45–60 minutes, selected letters involving secrecy, coded language, intelligence sharing, warnings, or concerns about interception and betrayal.

STUDENT DISCUSSION GUIDE

High School Track

1. Why were letters especially dangerous during wartime?

2. What evidence suggests writers were worried about being read by others?

3. How does secrecy change the way writers communicate information?

University Track

1. How do these letters function as tools of intelligence as well as personal communication?

2. In what ways does fear of interception shape tone, language, and omission?

3. How does trust operate under conditions of surveillance and uncertainty?

INSTRUCTOR NOTES

This unit highlights the importance of information control during the Revolutionary era. Letters reveal how intelligence depended not only on courage, but on discretion, silence, and trust between individuals.

Optional enrichment activities support independent and online learners while offering opportunities for deeper analysis in undergraduate courses. Instructors may emphasize espionage networks, the ethics of secrecy, or the fragility of trust during wartime.

This unit reinforces the idea that communication itself became a battlefield during the Revolution.

REQUIRED CORE ANALYSIS ACTIVITY

Secrecy as Historical Evidence

Students select one letter and analyze it using the following framework:

- What information is shared carefully or indirectly?

- What information is omitted, disguised, or hinted at?

- What risks does the writer acknowledge or imply?

- How does secrecy affect trust between writer and recipient?

Students should support their analysis with specific language from the letter.

OPTIONAL EXPERIENTIAL ENRICHMENT

Communication, Codes, and Risk

This enrichment explores how secrecy and trust operated in everyday communication. Cooking is never required.

Option A — Independent /At-Home

(Homeschool, Online, Independent Study)

Students complete one of the following activities:

Choice 1: Coded Message Exercise

- Rewrite a short passage from a letter as if the writer feared interception.

- Explain what information was hidden or altered and why.

Choice 2: Trust Reflection

- Write a reflection answering:

  What makes communication trustworthy when secrecy is necessary?

Option B — Instructor-Led / Group

(In-Person, Hybrid, or Seminar Courses)

Students may:

- Analyze letters for indirect language or warnings

- Discuss the risks of sharing information during wartime

- Examine how secrecy shaped relationships and decision-making

Activities may be discussion-based and do not require reenactment.

ASSESSMENT OPTIONS

High School Track

- Short essay: *Why secrecy mattered during the American Revolution*

- Primary-source response focused on communication and risk

University Track

- Analytical paper on espionage and information networks

- Seminar discussion on leadership, secrecy, and trust as wartime strategies

UNIT 6 LEARNING OUTCOMES

By the end of this unit, students should be able to:

- Explain the role of secrecy and intelligence in the Revolutionary War

- Analyze letters as instruments of both communication and strategy

- Interpret indirect language as historical evidence

- Understand trust as a critical and fragile wartime resource

UNIT 7

AFTERMATH, MEMORY, AND MEANING

Historical Focus

- The personal aftermath of the Revolutionary War

- Loss, return, and rebuilding

- Memory, meaning, and reflection

- Whose voices endure and whose are lost

- The gap between victory and lived reality

Instructional Note

This unit encourages students to examine how individuals processed the end of the war and how personal memory contributes to historical meaning beyond formal victory narratives.

Suggested Listening

Approximately 45–60 minutes, selected letters reflecting on loss, return, reflection, rebuilding, and the long-term impact of the Revolutionary War.

STUDENT DISCUSSION GUIDE

High School Track

1. How do writers describe life after the war compared to life during it?

2. What emotions appear most strongly in letters written after major fighting ends?

3. Do these letters suggest closure, or continued struggle? Explain.

University Track

1. How do these letters complicate traditional narratives of triumph and independence?

2. In what ways does memory shape the meaning of the Revolution for those who lived it?

3. Whose voices appear most often in postwar letters, and whose are absent?

INSTRUCTOR NOTES

This unit invites students to reflect on the long-term human consequences of the Revolution. Letters provide insight into how individuals understood sacrifice, loss, and survival after formal conflict ended.

Optional enrichment activities support independent and online learners while offering opportunities for deeper analysis in undergraduate settings. Instructors may emphasize memory, narrative construction, or the limits of historical closure.

This unit reinforces the understanding that historical meaning emerges over time and is shaped by personal experience as much as political outcome.

REQUIRED CORE ANALYSIS ACTIVITY

Memory as Historical Evidence

Students select one letter and analyze it using the following framework:

- What experiences does the writer reflect upon?

- How does the writer describe loss, survival, or change?

- What meaning does the writer assign to the war's outcome?

- How does memory influence tone and interpretation?

Students should support their analysis with specific language from the letter.

OPTIONAL EXPERIENTIAL ENRICHMENT

Reflection, Legacy, and Continuity

This enrichment supports reflective engagement with postwar life and memory. Cooking is never required.

Option A — Independent / At-Home

(Homeschool, Online, Independent Study)

Students complete one of the following activities:

Choice 1: Legacy Letter

- Write a letter from the perspective of a Revolutionary-era individual reflecting on the war years later.

- Base the reflection on themes and language found in the letters studied.

Choice 2: Memory Mapping

- Create a written reflection tracing how the meaning of the Revolution changes across letters from wartime to postwar periods.

Option B — Instructor-Led / Group

(In-Person, Hybrid, or Seminar Courses)

Students may:

- Compare wartime and postwar letters

- Discuss how memory shapes historical narratives

- Examine how silence and absence affect historical understanding

Activities may be discussion-based and do not require reenactment.

ASSESSMENT OPTIONS

High School Track

- Reflective essay: *How individuals experienced the aftermath of the American Revolution*

- Primary-source response focused on memory and meaning

University Track

- Analytical paper on memory as a historical source

- Seminar discussion on leadership on postwar identity and meaning

UNIT 7 LEARNING OUTCOMES

By the end of this unit, students should be able to:

- Analyze letters as reflections on memory and aftermath

- Explain how meaning evolves after conflict ends

- Interpret personal correspondence as long-term historical evidence

- Recognize the limits of victory narratives in lived experience

UNIT 8

LEGACY, MEMORY, AND THE RESPONSIBILITY

OF HISTORY

This final unit and curriculum conclusion are designed to support educators who are guiding students through *The Lost Letters of the American Revolution* as a primary-source learning experience.

Unlike traditional survey histories, this curriculum positions students not as passive recipients of historical knowledge but as active interpreters, ethical readers, and future stewards of memory. Unit 8 and the concluding sections invite learners to step beyond analysis and into responsibility.

This material is appropriate for:

- Upper-level High School Track history courses

- Homeschool learners seeking transcript-worthy work

- Undergraduate history, humanities, American studies, or public history programs

- Community education, museum education, and lifelong learning programs

Educators are encouraged to adapt the pacing and depth to learners' levels, while maintaining the core emphasis on primary sources, lived experience, and historical accountability.

UNIT OVERVIEW

Unit 8 asks students to confront a central question of historical study: What responsibility do we have once forgotten voices are recovered?

After analyzing letters, objects, foodways, and lived experiences, learners now reflect on how history is remembered, who gets remembered, and why it matters today.

This unit bridges academic inquiry with ethical reflection, helping students understand that history is not static—it is curated, interpreted, and passed forward.

LEARNING OBJECTIVES

By the end of Unit 8, students will be able to:

- Explain how historical narratives are shaped by preservation, loss, and power

- Analyze whose voices were excluded from traditional Revolutionary histories

- Reflect on the modern responsibility of historians, educators, and readers

- Connect primary-source study to contemporary civic memory and identity

- Articulate how ordinary lives shape national legacy

CORE THEMES

- History as memory, not myth

- Silence, absence, and archival gaps

- Who decides what is preserved

- The role of the reader as witness

- History as an ongoing conversation

PRIMARY SOURCE FOCUS

Students revisit selected letters from *The Lost Letters of the American Revolution* with a new lens:

- Letters that were never meant to survive

- Voices that were never meant to lead

- Lives that mattered without recognition

Rather than analyzing for facts alone, students now examine meaning, omission, and consequence.

KEY DISCUSSION QUESTIONS

- What stories survive, and which disappear?

- How does the survival of a document shape our understanding of the past?

- Is history incomplete by nature—or by choice?

- What changes when we create ordinary voices instead of famous ones?

- What responsibility do we carry after learning this history?

EXPERIENTIAL LEARNING OPTIONS

For Homeschool & Independent Learners

- Create a "Letter to the Future" reflecting what you would want remembered about today.

- Curate a small family or community artifact and document its story

- Interview a living relative and preserve their story as a primary source

For Classrooms & Groups

- Archival ethics debate: What deserves preservation?

- Group curation project: Build a "People's Archive" of overlooked voices

- Reflective journaling on memory, silence, and historical justice

WRITING & REFLECTION ASSIGNMENT

Choose One:

- Reflective Essay: *Why Ordinary Voices Matter in History*

- Creative Nonfiction: A modern response to a Revolutionary letter

- Civic Reflection: How historical memory influences modern identity

All assignments emphasize clarity, empathy, and historical grounding.

ASSESSMENT CRITERIA

Students are evaluated on:

- Depth of reflection

- Connection to primary sources

- Historical awareness and responsibility

- Thoughtful engagement with memory and legacy

This curriculum began with letters—private words never intended for public memory.

Through careful reading, contextual analysis, material culture study, and experiential learning, students have uncovered not only historical facts but human lives embedded within them. By the end of this journey, learners should understand a central truth:

History is not only what survives. History is what we choose to remember.

The American Revolution was not lived solely by founders, generals, or statesmen. It was lived by laborers, messengers, women, apprentices, farmers, enslaved people, and families whose voices were often lost to time. *The Lost Letters of the American*

Revolution restores those voices—not as curiosities, but as essential threads of the American story.

This curriculum intentionally closes not with mastery, but with reflection. Students are asked to consider how memory is shaped, how silence functions, and how modern readers inherit responsibility once forgotten voices are recovered.

The work of history does not end here. It continues through preservation, teaching, ethical storytelling, and civic engagement.

College-Level Capstone Project: Legacy & Memory

CAPSTONE PROJECT OVERVIEW (COLLEGE & ADVANCED LEARNERS)

The Capstone Project serves as a culminating academic experience for undergraduate or advanced learners. It requires students to synthesize primary-source analysis, historical context, and ethical reflection into a meaningful final work.

This project is suitable for:

- Undergraduate history courses

- Honors programs

- Independent study credits

- Public history or museum studies pathways

CAPSTONE PROJECT OPTIONS

Students must complete ONE option.

Option 1: Research & Interpretation Paper

A 12–15-page analytical paper centered on a theme from *The Lost Letters of the American Revolution* (e.g., memory, labor, domestic life, communication, silence in archives).

Option 2: Public History Project

Design a public-facing history project, such as:

- A digital exhibit

- A museum-style interpretive panel series

- An educational website or archive

- A curriculum or lesson plan for secondary learners

Option 3: Archival Ethics & Memory Essay

A reflective scholarly essay examining:

- Who controls historical memory

- Ethical responsibilities of historians

- The consequences of archival silence

CAPSTONE LEARNING OUTCOMES

Students completing the capstone will demonstrate:

- Mastery of primary-source interpretation

- Strong historical writing and argumentation

- Ethical awareness of memory and preservation

- Ability to translate historical research into modern relevance

Legacy Project Rubric (Required for Completion)

LEGACY PROJECT EVALUATION RUBRIC

Projects are evaluated using the following criteria:

1. Historical Accuracy & Source Use

- Effective use of primary sources
- Accurate historical context
- Clear Citation Practices

2. Depth of Analysis

- Thoughtful interpretation beyond surface-level facts
- Engagement with memory, omission, and legacy

3. Ethical Awareness

- Consideration of historical responsibility
- Awareness of whose voices are centered or absent

4. Clarity & Presentation

- Clear organization and communication
- Appropriate academic or public-facing tone

5. Original Insight

- Independent thought
- Meaningful contribution to historical understanding